635.9
GILB

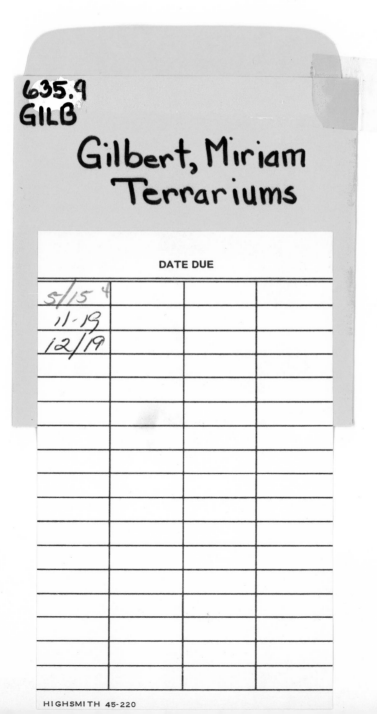

635.9
GILB

Gilbert, Miriam
Terrariums

DATE DUE			
5/15			
11-19			
12/19			

HIGHSMITH 45-220

Science-Hobby Book of
Terrariums

Science-Hobby Book of
Terrariums

by
MIRIAM GILBERT

ILLUSTRATED BY **WALTER FERGUSON**

ELIZABETH L. HAMMELL

CHARLES J. MAZOUJIAN

ISABELLE REID

Published by
LERNER PUBLICATIONS COMPANY
Minneapolis, Minnesota

To MY SISTER
because
she's my sister

Second Printing 1971

Revised edition copyright © 1968 by Lerner Publications Company
Original copyright © MCMLXI by Hammond Incorporated

International Standard Book Number: 0-8225-0558-4
Library of Congress Catalog Card Number: 68-54181

Manufactured in the United States of America

LIZARD   Lilo Hess-Three Lions, Inc.

Foreword

What kind of nature enthusiast are you?

Are you the kind who likes to hike through fields and woods, along streams and lakes to find out about nature first hand? Are you the kind who likes to set up exhibits of live things such as fish and reptiles and growing plants, or to make collections of inanimate things such as rocks and shells and pressed flowers? Or are you possibly the kind who prefers to sit quietly at home reading about nature?

To become a real naturalist you need to be all three kinds.

By getting out into nature you'll see how plants grow, how animals live, and find out how plants and animals depend on each other. By bringing home specimens you'll have a chance to study them at leisure and in close detail. And then, reading about them, you will find out the correct names for what you have seen and collected and will learn what other naturalists have discovered about them.

By going about your nature pursuits in this way, you will pick up a science hobby that will give you hours and days of enjoyment for the rest of your life. But not only that: you will learn to use your eyes to *observe* things, your mind to *figure out* things, and your hands to *do* things — three very important parts of the training of a budding scientist.

WILLIAM HILLCOURT
Author of BOY SCOUT HANDBOOK and
FIELD BOOK OF NATURE ACTIVITIES AND CONSERVATION

CONTENTS

A WOODLAND TERRARIUM   Ernst G. Hofmann

Starting
A Terrarium

WHAT IS A TERRARIUM?

A terrarium may be defined simply as a glass-enclosed garden. It may contain plants only or both plants and animals. Usually a terrarium is made out of a container with glass and screen sides, a glass or screen top which may be lifted off, and a bottom layer of sand or soil, containing plants.

But a terrarium is much more than this. It can be the window through which you enjoy seeing nature close at hand. It will help you to understand the way animals live and how interdependent — and independent — they are. It will give you a greater appreciation of many living things. Snakes, for example, which some people view with distaste, make fascinating terrarium pets. You can see the forces of nature at work.

Three of the common classifications of terrariums, based on the natural habitat of the plants and animals, are woodland, desert and semi-aquatic. The kind of pets you keep and the kind of plants you include determine the kind of terrarium you set up.

A variety of containers can be improvised for terrariums. Plastic dishes, glass jars and such have been successfully used. Serious hobbyists, after experimenting, however, generally recommend a 10-gallon or larger aquarium tank, at least 18 inches long, 13 inches wide and 12 inches high. If possible, buy a larger size in order to accommodate more plants and animals.

A terrarium for both plants and animals should have the top and one side (or part of one side) made of screen. No animal can feel comfortable if he is "boxed in." A desert terrarium containing plants only needs no cover.

Here are some of the conditions you should strive to create and a few of the animals and plants that go in each type of terrarium.

WOODLAND TERRARIUM

KIND OF ANIMALS

You have a wide range of animals from which to choose. This includes chameleons, snakes, such as garter snakes, toads, wood and cricket frogs and the box and wood turtles, which are land turtles.

SETTING UP

Prepare a bottom layer of coarse sand or gravel, 1-2 inches deep. Cover with a 2-3 inch layer of leaf mold or humus. Some terrarium owners put a ¼ inch layer of charcoal or small pebbles in between the sand and soil for drainage and to keep the soil sweet, but this is optional. Soak the gravel layer with water that has been allowed to age by standing in an open jar for several days. Keep the top layer moist, but not saturated.

KIND OF PLANTS

In furnishing your terrarium with plant life, remember your aim is to capture a miniature of nature. Work out a multi-leveled landscaping scene. Include an assortment of woodland trimmings, such as acorns and odd shaped rocks. Flat rocks can create the illusion of ledges, and a few stones artfully piled together make a cave.

The choice of plants for a woodland terrarium is almost unlimited. You can find a wide profusion of suitable ferns, mosses and other small plants on a walk through the woods. Of course, you can supplement the specimens you gather with any store-bought plants you may want to add for decorative touches. For example, if moss is not available from the woods, sphagnum moss may be used. This is dry and can be purchased from your florist. When you are ready to look for woodland plants, observe which ones go together in their natural setting. This will help you work out your own plant arrangement in a similar manner.

Materials for setting up a terrarium   B. H. Amlick

WINTERGREEN

Often used in a
woodland terrarium

POINTERS FOR GATHERING PLANTS

Do not take more plants than you need. Choose plants that will fit
easily into the size and shape of the container you plan to use. Select
plants that blend well with one another. Do not uproot a single plant
standing by itself. If there are apparently only two plants of the same type
in an area, dig up just one. Observe the elementary laws of conservation.
When gathering your plants, fold each one in a paper towel before putting
it in a box.

TOOLS NEEDED TO GATHER PLANTS

The following will be useful: heavy kitchen knife. You will need this
to cut around the plants. A trowel, pancake turner and broad-bladed putty
knife or spatula to help in gathering mosses.

COMMON WOODLAND TERRARIUM PLANTS

FERNS: Maidenhair *Adiantum cuneatum,* ebony spleenwort *Asplenium platy-
neuron,* Christmas fern *Polystichum acrostichoides,* which stays green winter
and summer, also *Woodsia obtusia, Woodsia scopulina* and walking fern
Camptosorus rhizophyllus.

MOSSES: Low-growing mosses provide wall-to-wall carpeting for your terrarium. They also make attractive linings for the sides of your container.
They can be easily cut and shaped.

Club mosses are more closely related to the ferns than to the mosses
but their long stems spread out to make them a good ground cover. Among
the varieties which terrarium owners recommend are: shining club moss
Lycopodium lucidulum and tree club moss *Lycopodium obscurum.*

LIVERWORTS: Small green plants similar to the mosses. They get their odd
name because the main leaf-like part of the plant resembles the human liver.

FUNGI: A group of plants that lack chlorophyll and so have no green coloring, and cannot manufacture their own food. They exist by absorbing ingredients from whatever they grow on. When gathering, take the fungi on the stick or piece of bark to which they are attached.

LICHENS: are part fungi and part algæ which live symbiotically. The fungi gets food material from the cells of the algæ; the algæ, in recompense, are protected and kept moist by the fungi. Thus, lichens are able to grow on rocks and other open areas, where they would not survive normally.

LOW-GROWING PLANTS AND VINES: The following plants are among the infinite variety which you can use: babys' tears *Helxine soleirdi* is a low, bright green, creeping, moss-like plant. Wax begonia *Begonia semperflorens* comes in many varieties, some with ornamental flowers, averages about 1 to 2 feet tall with foliage, in silver, pink, red, varying shades of green; also spotted or banded. Creeping fig *Ficus pumila* is an evergreen creeper with small leaves. Partridge berry *Mitchella repens,* an evergreen trailer, with dark green leaves, is colorful all the year round. In the spring, the ends of each branch blossom out with delicately pink or white flowers. These flowers are followed by scarlet berries, which usually survive through the winter, making this plant popular at Christmas as a holiday decoration. Strawberry-geranium *Saxifraga sarmentosa* is a trailing plant that bears white flowers. It owes its interesting name to the fact that it propagates itself by means of runners in the same way as the strawberry plant.

SHRUBS AND TREES: Tiny shrubs and young trees that are first starting to sprout from seeds (seedlings) may be used in a woodland terrarium. Cedar, white pine and hemlock are highly rated varieties in the evergreen family. Seedlings from oak, maple and birch trees will also grow in a woodland terrarium. Remove them when they become tall.

PARTRIDGE BERRY
Mitchella repens

Setting up a
woodland terrarium

Ernst G. Hofmann

STEPS IN PLANTING A WOODLAND TERRARIUM

Cut a thin piece of moss with scissors. Remove any bits of dirt with tweezers. Line the bottom and sides of the container with the moss. Shape in a varied, split-level contour. Arrange rocks to continue the landscaping scheme. Include a few large rocks which will not be obscured by the plants. Moisten moss slightly. Give plant tops a bath. Dip in a dish of water to loosen dirt. Remove dead leaves. Use a pencil to poke holes in the earth for the plants. Set plants in their holes. Cover with humus, anchoring plants firmly. Spray the plants lightly with water. A rubber bulb with a spray attachment is excellent for this purpose. Let the earth soak up the water. Give enough, but not too much water. You will know you have watered adequately if a bit of moisture comes out when pressed down with your finger. When planting is finished, wipe the terrarium glass clean with a lint-free towel or a paper towel.

TEMPERATURE

Daytime: 70-75° F. Nighttime: 50-60° F. Sunlight: An hour or two of early morning or late afternoon sunlight. The greatest part of the day, place the woodland terrarium in a semi-shaded spot.

DESERT OR ARID TERRARIUM

KIND OF ANIMALS

Lizards, including the Texas horned lizard and collared lizard; non-poisonous snakes from the desert regions in the West and Southwest and other harmless, warm-and-dry area inhabitants, such as the gopher tortoise are suitable for a desert terrarium.

SETTING UP

Mix fine sand with soil. Fill the terrarium to a depth of approximately 2 inches with this mixture.

KIND OF PLANTS

Small cacti, succulents, aloes, agaves, may be used. Small cacti, with their flowerpots, may be buried directly in the sand.

Don't neglect the watering of a desert terrarium. Lightly spray plants and the sand, about once a week, using a rubber bulb sprinkler. A good guide is to keep the bottom layer of sand moist, and the top dry. A small shallow dish of water should be set up for the animals, in one corner of the terrarium.

TEMPERATURE

Daytime: 75-85° F. Nighttime: Not lower than 65° F. Sunlight: Desert denizens enjoy long hours of sunshine. They need sunshine, especially during the winter months, but use discretion. Create shady hide-aways within the terrarium, with plant and rock formations, where desert animals can find shelter from the sun. During cold spells, it may be necessary to keep an electric bulb, shielded with a reflector, shining over the top of the terrarium to provide an extra safety measure of warmth. If possible, situate the bulb so that the animals have a chance to move away to a cooler area, if they prefer. If the terrarium is small, keep the light on only for short periods.

SEMI-AQUATIC TERRARIUM

KIND OF ANIMALS

A wide variety of frogs, ranging from the large bullfrog to the common leopard frog, salamanders and newts, small turtles and baby alligators.

SETTING UP

Section off about three-quarters of the bottom for a dry area, leaving the remainder as a water area.

The kind of animals you plan to put in the semi-aquatic terrarium determines how large or small a water area you provide. Toads, wood frogs, tree frogs and some of the salamanders are content with a terrarium that has a few inches of water at one end of the tank, and even a small dish of water will suffice. Turtles, alligators, bullfrogs and green frogs prefer a large pool of water.

There are several ways to partition off the water section from the lands. Two methods which are commonly used are:

1. Set a shallow square dish in the soil for the water area. Sand, gravel and plants may be arranged around the rim of the dish so there is no abrupt demarcation between the land and water.

2. Place a strip of glass, slate or thin board across the bottom of the terrarium to hold back the earth and create space for a pond. A few rocks, with a handful of pebbles, should be piled near one edge of the pool to help the animals crawl out. By graduating the stones in a slight incline on the water side, you can partially obscure the dividing strip and add to a more natural impression.

KIND OF PLANTS
The same as for the woodland terrarium.

TEMPERATURE
Daytime: 70-75° F. Nighttime: Not lower than 60° F. Sunlight: Avoid direct mid-day sun. Window shades or curtains should be drawn during the hottest part of the day to soften the sun's rays. As a precaution, use a thermometer to check on temperature fluctuations in the terrarium.

BOG TERRARIUM
An interesting variation of the semi-aquatic terrarium is the bog terrarium, which requires the kind of acid soil found in a bog or swamp. The animals are the same as would be used in the semi-aquatic terrarium, and the enclosure, covered with a slightly elevated glass top, is the same type. The acidity of the soil lends itself to some fascinating plant species, such as the insect-devouring Sundew, Venus flytrap and the small Pitcher plant. A few fruit flies set loose in the bog terrarium will soon be snapped up by plants of this type.

SETTING UP
The bottom layer consists of gravel, which is then covered with 2-3 inches of bog soil. The acidity of the soil presents a challenge in setting up and maintaining a bog terrarium. Plants need to be lightly sprayed every few days with a non-alkaline water. Rain water is your best source if your usual

Plants suitable for a desert terrarium   B. H. Amlick

A DESERT TERRARIUM   Ernst G. Hofmann

supply of water is alkaline. One way to test for water alkalinity is to use red litmus paper. The dye used in it is derived from certain lichens. What happens is that red litmus paper turns blue from excess alkali. Thus, in checking your water supply, if the red litmus paper turns blue, you know the water is alkaline. You can make water acid by adding acetic acid (vinegar) to it. Blue litmus paper it used to test for water acidity. When the blue litmus paper turns red, the water is acid and is therefore usable in a bog terrarium.

WHAT ARE AMPHIBIANS?

Amphibians and reptiles are often grouped together but each class has its own interesting characteristics and deserves to be considered separately. The study of amphibians and reptiles is called herpetology. The study of amphibians alone is called amphibiology.

Amphibians are animals which spend part of their lives in the water and part on land. These are the animals which hundreds of millions of years ago came out of the water to live on land. Thus in the evolutionary process, they are considered a bridge between the fish and the reptiles. The Greek word *Amphibios,* meaning "living a double life," is indicative of this land and water development. Amphibians are divided into: frogs and toads, salamanders and cæcilians. There are certain differences among these three groups.

1. Frogs and toads when fully grown are tailless. Their hind legs are well developed for jumping.

2. Salamanders have tails and legs.

3. Cæcilians are burrowing, worm-like animals, with no legs. Their habitat is the tropics.

A SEMI-AQUATIC TERRARIUM   Ernst G. Hofmann

Some of the similarities of these groups are:

1. Each undergoes a striking change of appearance as it develops. Frogs and toads, for example, pass through the egg and larva stage before becoming mature.

2. Each usually changes its habitat as it changes its form. The larvæ, which breathe by means of gills, live in the water most of the time. Adults, which develop lungs, generally become land animals. They often complete the cycle by returning to the water to breed.

Other interesting characteristics of amphibians are:

1. They are vertebrates; that is, they have a backbone.

2. They are cold-blooded. Their body temperature varies with atmospheric conditions, rising or falling as the outside temperature rises or falls. By contrast, warm-blooded animals maintain a body temperature, independent of atmospheric fluctuations. Thus, the temperature of the atmosphere plays a vital role in controlling the health of amphibians in a terrarium. Severe cold or excessive heat can kill them. This irregularity in body temperature explains why these animals hibernate in winter and estivate in summer. This must be taken into account when setting up a terrarium. If you maintain an even and warm temperature during the winter months, the amphibians will be discouraged from hibernating. Since amphibians are cold-blooded, they are usually found in the warmer areas of the world, where they can survive more readily.

3. Amphibians are carnivorous and swallow their food whole. This should be taken into consideration when feeding frogs and toads since food should not be offered them which is too large.

FROGS

Frogs make good terrarium pets. Some frogs have been known to live as long as 25 to 30 years when properly cared for in a terrarium. You may use different varieties of frogs in your terrarium as long as they are about the same size. Big frogs often attack smaller ones.

Frogs will eat almost any kind of living insect: grasshoppers, beetles, worms, moths, house-flies, spiders, caterpillars and earthworms. In the winter when insects are hard to find, a frog may be fed meal worms or meal bugs. Frogs will also eat raw meat, such as liver, hamburger and lean beef. Occasionally a piece of hard cheese can be given to vary the diet.

Frogs pay little or no attention to food which is not moving since they are used to catching living insects. The way to feed your frog is to put a bit of meat on the end of a broomstraw or toothpick and dangle it in front of the frog. Some terrarium owners put a snip of meat on the end of a thread or string and sway it in the air. Be sure that the meat will come off the thread easily. Also, hold the food a short distance away as the position of the frog's eyes makes it difficult to see anything that is too close to it.

CATCHING A FROG

Frogs live in many parts of the countryside. They may be found near damp areas, such as ponds, swamps and marshes, as well as in the woods or meadows.

The best time to hunt for frogs is at night. The best season is during the spring and summer, which is the usual mating season. Take along a flashlight. When you spot a likely specimen, use your flashlight, held securely in one hand, to dazzle the frog. With your free hand, pounce for the frog and grasp it by its hind legs, before it has a chance to recover from its momentary blindness.

If you are frog-hunting during the day, try attracting the frog's attention by moving your hand in front of it, then make a dash for it by the hind legs. You've got to hop to it if you want to play a game of leapfrog with a frog.

You can carry the frog home in a net or cotton bag. It does not need water if you are going only a short distance. But you must not deprive the frog of water for any length of time. You can also use a can with a cover, or a jar partly filled with water to bring your frog home.

FROGS' EGGS

Instead of catching a frog, you may want to gather frogs' eggs and watch them develop. It is a fascinating experience to observe the life cycle of an animal, especially your own pet.

From early spring until summer is the time to collect frogs' eggs. In those southern states having a warmer temperature, you may be able to gather frogs' eggs toward the end of winter and sometimes even in midwinter. You will find frogs' eggs on plant stems or leaves in shallow water along the shore, or floating in masses on top of the water. They look like dark pencil dots in a jelly covering.

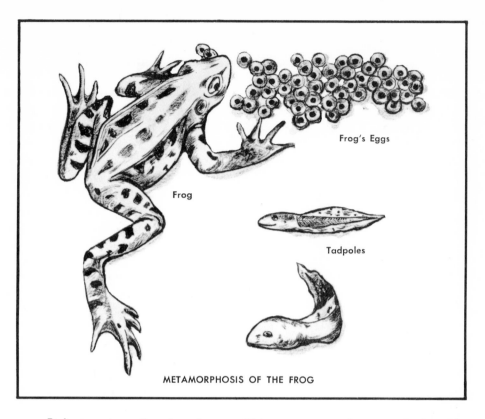

Frog's Eggs

Frog

Tadpoles

METAMORPHOSIS OF THE FROG

It is easy to gather frogs' eggs. Using a net, gently sweep it through the shallow part of the pond. Scoop the eggs into a glass jar or pail partly filled with some of the pond water. You can work without a net, too. Place a glass jar, filled with some of the pond water, under the eggs and lift the eggs into the container.

If the jar is large enough, the frogs' eggs can hatch in the uncovered jar, or you may transfer them to an aquarium, glass bowl or enameled basin, if you prefer. Always be sure to use the pond water where you found the eggs. Place them where they will have about two to three hours of sun daily. The length of hatching time depends upon the temperature of the water and the species of the frog which laid the eggs. It may be from a few days to a few weeks. Do not be impatient. A sign of trouble is the egg mass turning white. This means that the eggs are not developing.

TADPOLES

You may want to gather your frog specimens at different levels of their development. If you would like to catch some tadpoles, hunt in the same shallow pond areas where the frogs lay their eggs. You can use a small-meshed net to help catch these wriggling fellows.

Tadpoles are interesting terrarium pets. Some change into frogs in a few months, others take longer. Some are so small, you can hardly see them; others, such as the tadpole of the bullfrog, may measure as much as 3 to 4 inches in length when they are born.

Tadpoles in the process of changing into frogs should be kept in a semi-aquatic terrarium with growing plants. Tadpoles thrive on the algæ which forms on the plant leaves and on the glass sides of the tank.

Newly hatched tadpoles can be fed greens, such as bits of raw lettuce or spinach. They will also eat tiny, crumbled-up pieces of hard-boiled egg yolk. Larger tadpoles will eat small slivers of raw liver or fish and prepared fish food.

When it first hatches, the tadpole is a tiny, flat-looking squiggle. It has a pair of gills on the sides of its neck with which it breathes the air in the water like a fish. It has a long tail and a round body. Gradually the metamorphosis of the tadpole into the frog takes place. The body changes. The gills grow smaller and lungs start to form. The legs and arms develop. The tail shrinks until it finally disappears and the young frog emerges.

There are 2,000 different kinds of frogs. The BULLFROG is the largest American frog; the TREE FROGS include some of our smallest varieties. The bullfrog *Rana catesbeiana,* when fully grown, can measure from 6 to 8 inches, not counting its long legs. Bullfrogs are famous for their jumping prowess. Some cities have held jumping-frog contests and it is recorded that a bullfrog can cover as much as five feet per jump! Mark Twain immortalized the jumping frog in his story, "The Celebrated Jumping Frog of Calaveras County."

Bullfrogs never sing in chorus as most frogs do. Their call is a solitary one. It's supposed to sound like: "bottle-o'-rum, jug-o'-rum, more rum." The timbre of its voice is so deep that it has been compared to a bull and on a clear night the resonant bullfrog boom can be heard a great distance away.

Bullfrogs have a green head with a green or greenish-brown body. The under parts are yellowish-white. Some varieties found in the Gulf states are dark on top, almost black in color and mottled underneath.

Bullfrogs are cannibalistic and will eat small fish, newts, young snakes and salamanders. It is safest, therefore, to set up a bullfrog as king of his own domain unless you include in the same terrarium an adult water snake, garter snake or other animals which would be too uncomfortably large for the bullfrog to swallow. The bullfrog does best in a terrarium with a large swimming pool partitioned from the dry land.

Green frog *Rana clamitans,* which comes bedecked in a vivid green on its head and shoulders, is another large frog. It is smaller than the bullfrog, however, averaging about 4 inches, but has several similarities. It is cannabilistic and enjoys the same diet of small live frogs, salamanders and newts. It needs a large water area in a semi-aquatic terrarium.

Leopard and pickerel frogs *Rana pipiens* and *Rana palustris* are other frogs which are perfectly suited for the semi-aquatic terrarium since in their natural habitat, they live equally well on land or in the water.

The leopard frog, which is found widely scattered throughout the United States, is our most common frog. The two species are often mistaken for one another because of the leopard-like spots on their back. However, there are differences in shape of spots and coloring between the two. The leopard frog has smaller, rounder spots, which are ringed round in white. The back is

TREE FROG
Hyla versicolor

usually green or brownish. The underparts are white. The pickerel frog has squarish spots in a more regular pattern on a gray or grayish-green body. Both species average about 2-4 inches long. They are alert and hop about very actively.

Wood frog *Rana sylvatica* is another lively pet. It adapts well to a woodland terrarium since it lives in moist woods. It is small, 2-3 inches long, and comes in an attractive reddish-brown coloring.

Tree frog *Hyla versicolor* is sometimes known as tree toad because it is closely related to the toads but is smaller, averaging from ¾ to 2 inches. The tree frog adapts itself to either a woodland or a semi-aquatic terrarium. It has sticky pads on its toes which helps it to climb and cling to trees. The skin is usually brown or greenish, although it may vary in color and pattern. Its call is clear and musical in contrast to the deep reverberating boom of the bullfrog.

The green tree frog *Hyla cinerea,* (about 1½ to 2¼ inches) has a resonant bell-like call and has thus earned for itself the name "bell-frog" or "cowbell frog" in some areas. It can change its usual brilliant green color, which makes it an interesting pet to observe under varying conditions.

The spring peeper *Hyla crucifer* is even smaller than the green tree frog. It varies from ¾ to 1¼ inches. The spring peeper is not only one of the smallest of the tree frogs, it is among the smallest of all American frogs. It is light brown or gray in color with a dark diagonal cross on its back.

Cricket frog *Acris gryllus* is an interesting tree frog because unlike its relatives, it cannot climb trees! It lacks the usual adhesive toe pads characteristic of the tree frogs. Nature has compensated for this by endowing the cricket frog with remarkable leaping agility for a creature that averages no more

19

than an inch long. It should be kept in a large woodland terrarium where it will have ample space to jump about freely. Its color varies. Some are brown, grayish or an olive-green. The sharp, cricket-like call of the male in the spring accounts for its name.

Put a wooden ladder in your terrarium if you are going to include a tree frog. The tree frog has gained a reputation as a weather forecaster. If the tree frog stays on the ground, it's supposed to mean showers. If he climbs to the top of the ladder, sunshine is on its way. Whether you believe this or not, it's fun to see how many times your pet is right and how many times he's wrong. This superstition may have some foundation. It seems that the frog, reacting to atmospheric pressure, moves up or down.

Watching a frog change color is another fascinating phenomenon. It takes about an hour for the frog to change from green to gray or brown so don't give up too soon. The colors vary according to light and temperature. A dark cool place causes a frog's skin to darken. Sunlight and heat will make the skin take on a lighter hue.

TOADS

Toads are often grouped with frogs since, to the casual eye, they may seem the same. There are as many differences, however, as there are similarities between the two, and it is interesting for you to be able to distinguish between them.

In appearance, you will note the following differences between toads and frogs: Toads usually have dry, rougher skins. They are shorter and fatter than frogs. Toads' hind legs are shorter. Their eyes are larger. Toads have no teeth. In action, toads move more slowly and do not jump as far, as fast or as speedily as the frog.

As far as living habits are concerned, here too, they differ. Toads in general prefer to live in fields and gardens. Frogs prefer to live in or near water. Toads shun the sunlight, coming out mostly at night or in the late afternoon to hunt for food. Frogs, on the other hand, hunt for their food in the daytime as well as at night.

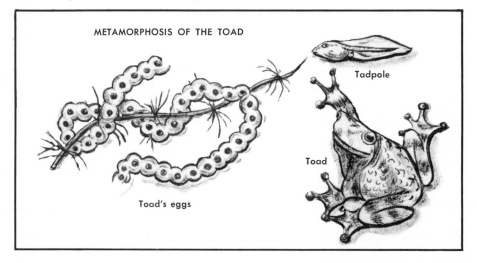

METAMORPHOSIS OF THE TOAD

Tadpole

Toad

Toad's eggs

COMMON TOAD
Bufo americanus

The toad's breeding habitat is similar to that of the frog since it lays its eggs in ponds or swamps. The eggs, however, are laid in long and string-like ropes and not deposited in a mass like frogs' eggs. It takes from three to twelve days before they become tadpoles. Toad tadpoles go through essentially the same metamorphosis as the frog tadpoles. After six to eight weeks, the tadpoles will be about ½ inch long. When the tadpoles develop into toads, they leave the ponds and seek out a home on land. It usually takes two to three years for toads to mature fully. Toads make good terrarium pets. They can be given the same type of diets as frogs. They enjoy fruit flies, small insects and tiny worms. Also, as in the case of frogs, you must give live food or else offer the food while it is in motion by dangling or swinging it in front of the toad.

Toads have several interesting characteristics. Their back which has warts of different sizes is the toad's protective suit of armor. The warts are tiny glands which contain a fluid, poisonous to animals but not to humans. When a toad is endangered by an animal or seized roughly, a poisonous substance is secreted by the warts, strong enough to make an animal sick and sometimes potent enought to kill an animal. This secretion cannot harm the human skin, or cause warts, as has often been said about toads. Should any get on you, however, wash it off immediately as it can be harmful to the eyes and irritating to the face.

Toads have another method of protecting themselves. They burrow away from an enemy. This may sound cowardly but it works out satisfactorily for the safety of the toad. The toad kicks backwards with its hind legs until it is practically buried under the earth. They look almost turtle-like since all that seems visible is the head. Should danger be scented, the head is popped under the dirt and the toad apparently disappears. Because of this habit, the soil in a woodland terrarium for toads should be loose and soft. Fowler's toad *Bufo fowleri,* named in honor of S. P. Fowler, a Massachusetts naturalist, is another eastern species. It is particularly common in the New England area. It is greener in coloration and smaller than the American toad. It is interesting that the female is larger than the male, averaging about 3 inches, while the male grows to be about 2 inches.

The smallest of the toads, in fact the smallest toad in the United States, is the oak toad *Bufo quercicus.* Its maximum size is about an inch and a quarter. It is widely found in Southern pine forests.

The toad's tongue is a tricky food-getting mechanism. It is attached at the front of the toad's mouth instead of at the back and it can be thrust forward and back so quickly that it is hardly visible. The tongue is sticky and as it flicks out, it catches its insect prey.

It is said that the toad drinks through its skin. In a way, this is true. The toad does not drink water by mouth. It get its water from the food it eats and absorbs moisture through its skin by soaking in water.

During the breeding season, which runs from April through July, the distinctive long-sustained, high pitched trill of the male can be clearly heard. When it sings, the male inflates its throat into a huge, light-colored sac, which blows up like a balloon. At breeding time, toads should be transferred to a terrarium of the semi-aquatic type. Otherwise, they should be housed in a woodland terrarium.

Since toads eat all sorts of harmful insects and bugs, which do costly vegetable and crop damage, the farmer welcomes the toad as a friend.

Some variety of the common toad is found from the Atlantic to the Pacific coast. The American toad *Bufo americanus,* which lives east of the Rocky Mountains, is the common eastern species. Its size varies from 2 to 4 inches in length.

A toad with its
bulging vocal sac

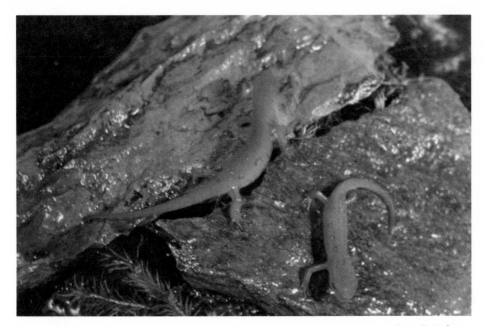

THE RED EFT   Ernst G. Hofmann

SALAMANDERS

Salamanders are closely related to frogs and may be kept successfully in terrariums in the same way as frogs and toads.

Salamanders live and breed in the same ponds and streams as frogs. They hatch from eggs which pass into the larval stage, then become adult salamanders. This is similar to the stages of development in a frog.

Just as frogs and toads are often mistaken for one another so salamanders are frequently confused with lizards. A fast glance at a salamander indicates why this is a natural error. The salamander's body is lizard-like and has a long tail. But on closer inspection, it will be seen that the skin is smooth while that of the lizard is scaly. The salamander's toes have no claws and they never have more than four toes on their front feet. Lizards usually have five. The salamander *Ambystoma tigrinum* and marbled salamander *Ambystoma opacum* get along well in a woodland terrarium. The tiger salamander is a hardy species and has been kept as a pet for 10 years or more. It is smooth-skinned, with a black body, marked with large yellow spots that seem to form bars, and which give it its colorful name. It attains a length of from 6-10 inches. In a terrarium, it usually is active at night and hides during the day.

It goes through the typical salamander growth progression. Early in spring, the eggs are laid. The eggs hatch into larvæ. According to Webster's Dictionary, "larvæ are the early form of any animal which while immature is unlike its parent and must pass through more or less of a metamorphosis

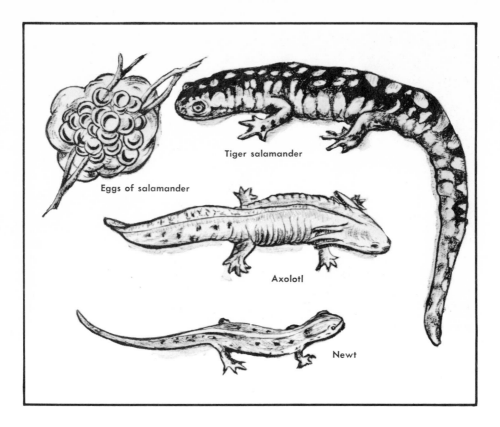

Eggs of salamander

Tiger salamander

Axolotl

Newt

before assuming the adult characters." This is exactly what happens. The salamander larvæ breathe through gills and remain in the water until they develop lungs, when they venture out onto land.

In some parts of the southwest, the tiger salamander retains its gills and does not leave the water. This type is known as the *Axolotl* and scientifically may be considered the permanent larvæ form.

Marbled salamander is closely related to the tiger salamander, but is smaller. Its maximum size is 5 inches. In appearance, it has the same type of body markings, except that the bars are white, on a dark gray or black background.

NEWTS are the most popular and playful of the salamanders for a terrarium. Newts go through unusual physical changes in their growth. There is such a complete change, at each level of development, that even the name of the animal changes.

Eastern pond or spotted newt *Diemictylus viridescens* is one of the salamanders encountered widely throughout the eastern states. In the early spring the eggs are laid on stems and leaves of water plants. When the eggs hatch into larvæ, the baby newts have tail-like appendages, are green and measure less than half an inch long. They live in the water, breathing by means of gills. At the end of two or three months, the tail is absorbed and lungs take the place of the gills. They then leave the ponds and streams and live on land for two or three years. During this period, they develop a bright red coat, and are known as the red eft. The eft favors moist woods. It secretes itself during the day lest its bright colors attract its enemies. When it reaches adulthood, it measures three to four inches long and its color changes to greenish-brown. But this isn't the end of Nature's remarkable legerdemain. The eft develops a swimming tail in its mature stage and returns to the water.

There are variations within this growth pattern. Sometimes, in certain habitats, the eft stage is by-passed; and occasionally in a home terrarium, the eft may not reach its aquatic adult stage for several years.

A semi-aquatic terrarium is ideal for newts since they can live in water or on land, according to their particular stage of development. Newts in the red eft stage can be placed in a woodland terrarium.

Salamanders and newts are easy to train and easy to feed. They will take bits of food from your fingers in time. They are carnivorous and prefer live insects, earthworms and meal worms but will also take raw fish or raw meat, such as chopped-up pieces of liver and hamburger. Like the frog, they respond more readily to food that moves. You may try to offer bits of raw meat on the end of a string, or on a toothpick. You can also drop the food in the water or put it on the dry land and they will come after it.

Baby newts should be fed every day but two feedings a week are sufficient for the adults. Do not over-stuff them. They will sometimes be fully satisfied with no more than three or four small mouthfuls.

Salamanders are inexpensive at a pet store but it's fun to go out on a salamander search and catch them instead of buying them. If you want to watch the entire metamorphosis of the salamander, hunt for salamander eggs, in the spring, in shallow ponds among water plants. The eggs are a jelly-like mass and look very much like the eggs of a frog. Scoop up the eggs with some pond water in a glass jar.

The salamander larvæ are found in the late spring and summer in ponds. They can be caught with a small net. Use a jar or a pail filled with pond water to carry them home. The adult salamander may be unearthed in damp areas in the woods in late summer or fall. A good time to look for them is in the early morning or soon after a rain when they usually come out of hiding. A likely place to find salamanders is under stones or logs. Catch the adult salamander in a small net or by hand. Do not reach for a salamander by the tail as it comes off easily.

The adult salamander may be carried home in a container with a small amount of water but it should have some sort of cover, either a netting of a lid with air holes in it.

Salamander eggs and the larvæ may be kept in an aquarium. The adult salamander and the maturing larvæ about to develop into the next stage of growth should be kept in a semi-aquatic terrarium.

WHAT ARE REPTILES?

Reptiles include four large groups: alligators and crocodiles, turtles, snakes and lizards. The tuatera, whose habitat is New Zealand, constitutes a rarely mentioned fifth category, because it is on the verge of extinction.

Reptiles are cold-blooded as are the amphibians but vary considerably in appearance from them. The skin of reptiles is dry and scaly which helps them to withstand heat. They are lung-breathing, sun-loving creatures. Most reptiles lay eggs from which the young are hatched. Some lizards and snakes, such as the garter snakes, ribbon snake and DeKay's, however, are vivaparous. This means that they produce their young alive.

The Texas horned lizard *Phrynosoma cornutum,* commonly nicknamed the horned "toad," is highly recommended for a desert terrarium. It is not a toad but a lizard with a short, thin tail. The term "toad," although a misnomer, is properly descriptive because it has a squat, toad-like shape. Its small, flat body (2½-4 inches in size) is covered with spiny scales. It has several defensive horn-like spikes on its head. Another defense mechanism is its singular ability to squirt blood from the corners of its eyes, which is caused by an increase of blood pressure in its forehead.

In a terrarium, the Texas horned lizard needs a few inches of dry sand and several hours of sunlight every day. It eats only when it is warm and must have a temperature of at least 70° F. or its health will deteriorate. Ants are its favorite diet but it will also eat meal worms, spiders and insect larvæ. It will not drink from a dish. It will quench its thirst, however, by lapping up, cat-like, drops of water from a lettuce leaf or low-growing plants, which should be sprinkled daily so that its thirst may be satisfied. It is diurnal in habit and most lively on bright, sunny days.

TEXAS HORNED LIZARD
Phrynosoma cornutum

AMERICAN "CHAMELEON"
(the common lizard)
A very popular
terrarium pet

Collared lizard *Crotaphytus collaris,* another desert creature from the southwest, is a spectacular terrarium specimen. Its double black collar, ringing the neck, is a distinctive marking but it is at breeding time that both the male and female species blossom out in vivid regalia. The male takes on a brilliant green, set off with yellow spots, and enhanced by an orange toned throat. Not to be outdone, preceding egg-laying, the female puts on a new red dress, with brighter hued spots of red, scattered over the limbs and tail.

The collared lizard has an odd way of running on its long, frog-like hind legs, in an erect position, with its forebody raised. It can get about with amazing swiftness in spite of its stout body and cumbersome appearing, large head.

It is belligerent in character and carnivorous and should be kept with lizards of its own size (average length is about 12 inches) since it will eat smaller lizards, snakes and horned toads.

American "chameleon" *Anolis carolinensis* is one of the lizard curiosities that can make owning a terrarium an exciting and enlightening experience.

True chameleons are not native to the United States. They are Old World lizards, found in large numbers in Madagascar, and ranging throughout Africa and Asia Minor, with a few species appearing in Europe.

27

OLD WORLD CHAMELEON
Lilo Hess-Three Lions, Inc.

The American "chameleon" is a common lizard, averaging from 5 to 7 inches in size. It is found in the coastal region of the southeast, from North Carolina to Florida, and as far west as Texas. Although names of animals are often misleading, they can also be revealing.

This popular terrarium lizard has rightfully earned its name because, like the chameleon, it does change its body color. The usual color is pale green. When it is excited, frightened or fighting, it dons a battling coat of brilliant green. At other times, when it is sleeping or resting, the color will become a subdued deep gray or brown. The layman's explanation that the lizard changes its color to adapt to its surroundings is only partly true. The scientific point-of-view is that changes in light, changes in temperature and changes in the lizard's emotional state produce a change in color.

It takes about three minutes for the American "chameleon" to change its color. It is a visual thrill which will hold you breathless each time you watch the subtle color transformation. First, the brown becomes a yellow; then the yellow fades into gray. Finally — and almost unbelievably — a green tone spreads and gradually deepens over the body. No artist could ever approximate this marvel of Nature's color palette and nothing can compare to seeing your own pet chameleon change color.

The American "chameleon" has adhesive toe pads, which enable it to walk about on all sorts of surfaces and in all kinds of tricky positions. It will have no trouble in walking up the glass sides of your terrarium, or hanging upside down from the top cover.

The males have an unusual throat pouch which hangs loosely under its lower jaw. When they prepare for courtship or combat, this dewlap expands fanlike into a bright display of color, ranging from red to pink, or orange to yellow. At the same time, they nod their heads in a serio-comic fashion. This is amusing to watch.

In a woodland terrarium, the American "chameleon" can be fed meal worms, insects and flies, which it especially relishes. If you want to have a supply of meal worms on hand, you can grow them yourself in bran or other flour, otherwise they are available at your pet shop. Water must be provided in the same manner as for the horned toad. The floor of the terrarium, preferably a moss bottom, and small plants should be sprinkled daily with a rubber bulb sprayer. In order to enjoy and encourage the antics of these frisky creatures, set up natural exercise equipment for them in the form of small trees or a branch firmly wedged in the soil.

You don't have to search for unusual lizards. The swifts, which belong to a large group of common lizards, will also enliven your terrarium.

The common swift or fence lizard *Sceloporus undulatus* divulges some of its traits through the nicknames which have been applied to it. It likes dry woods areas and is found in large numbers in pine forests, especially in the southeastern part of the United States, and is therefore also known as the "pine lizard." If you ever try to catch one, you will soon see why they deserve their name "swifts." They can also be spotted on fences and are sometimes called fence swifts. Not only are they fast, but clever, and catching one on your own can be a challenge. If you see one scurrying up the trunk of a tree and one moment he's there — and the next moment he has vanished — nine times out of ten, you will find him hiding on the other side of the trunk. This is a successful escapist trick used by squirrels and lizards, when they are being pursued. Catching a swift requires agility and skill on your part. Tracking down a likely specimen is half the job. Grabbing a lizard in just the right spot is the other half of the battle. Most lizards can shake off their tails and you may find yourself holding a wiggling tail while the lizard scoots off to safety. The tail-detaching maneuver is harmless to the lizard and in several weeks a new tail grows.

The fence lizard, which measures about 4-7 inches when fully grown, makes a good terrarium pet. It is hardy and will be content with a dry terrarium which receives good sunlight, for a home, and live flies and meal worms for a diet.

AMERICAN "CHAMELEON"
Anolis Carolinensis   Lilo Hess-Three Lions, Inc.

PINE TREE LIZARD
Sometimes it is called
the fence swift
Sceloporus undulatus

FACTS ABOUT SNAKES

We are sometimes afraid of things we know little about or sometimes we are misinformed and it is ignorance that breeds fear. This is true of snakes. Many bizarre notions have been spread about snakes that are not true. It will add to your fund of knowledge if you can help to correct some of the distortions of fact that are prevalent about snakes. As is so often the case, truth is stranger than fiction. You might be able to interest some of your friends in your hobby by sharing some of these curious facts about snakes with them.

Snakes do not have ear openings and so they are not sensitive to sounds in the air the way that we are. Their body acts as a sounding board and hears for them by picking up ground vibrations.

The snake has a tongue that "smells." Now that's one that will arouse your curiosity. But it's true. The tongue can't smell, in the usual sense. However, it does pick up objects which it carries to two small olfactory organs in the roof of its mouth. In this way, the tongue can help the snake to detect smells.

The eyes of a snake have a transparent lid which acts as a protective covering. The lid is immovable so that a snake sleeps with its eyes open. Thus, when you look at a motionless snake, you have no way of knowing for a certainty whether it is asleep or awake.

The way a snake eats is fascinating. Snakes have a large mouth and extensile jaws, which can stretch to swallow surprisingly large animals, due to the fact that the lower jaw consists of two separate parts, connected by an elastic ligament. Their teeth are too sharp for chewing and they swallow their food whole. This is why you can sometimes see the outline of food bulging inside a snake, when it is digesting its meal. The teeth (usually four rows on the top jaw, and two on bottom) slant back towards the throat and give them a hook-like grasp on their prey. Once an animal is caught, the more it struggles, the firmer it is gripped.

Snakes shed their skin at least once and sometimes several times a year. This is a natural, normal process and does not hurt the snake. It is comparable to a bird's molting and shedding its feathers.

When cold weather comes, a group of snakes of different varieties will often happen upon the same hibernating places and will "winter" together, in what is usually called a snake "den."

SNAKE TERRARIUM

A wooden container is usually recommended for a snake terrarium. You can make your own snake terrarium; the bottom, back and sides can be made of one-inch boards. The top should be of fine wire netting that is hinged or locks securely. One side should also be of fine wire netting to give cross ventilation. Check the box for any small openings since snakes are adept at squeezing through narrow spaces.

The base of a terrarium containing snakes must be kept dry. Some snakes are highly susceptible to skin infections and may even catch pneumonia, if the floor of the terrarium is wet. It is advisable to varnish the floor so that the wood will not absorb moisture. A layer of sand or gravel, 1½ inches deep, will also make a good dry bottom, or you may use several layers of newspaper, folded or cut to fit the floor of the terrarium to soak up excess moisture.

For your pond area, use a shallow glass dish, half filled with water. Set the dish firmly in one corner so that the water will not splash over onto the dry land. Also make sure the dish is sturdy and large enough for a snake to crawl into it without tipping it over.

The snake terrarium does not require direct sunlight. Do not make the mistake of giving your snakes too much sun, especially in summer. Avoid high temperatures as well. A range of between 65-80° F. is a good guide.

In setting up any terrarium, your aim is to duplicate nature in a small area. But imitation is not enough. Imagination is the plus factor that will make your terrarium a source of endless interest and delight to your family and friends.

Snakes demand very little to take care of their basic needs. Still it will add to your enjoyment, the beauty of your terrarium, and the health of your pets, if you do some creative landscaping.

In their natural environment, snakes like to conceal themselves among rocks and under leaf piles. Keep this habit in mind when planning your snake terrarium. You can set up scattered nooks by arranging some smooth stones to shape a cave or a semi-enclosure. A small box, turned upside down, with a hole cut in one end or a few dry leaves will also make good hide-and-seek places. If you will smooth and clean off a sturdy tree branch, and wedge it firmly in the gravel, it will add to the woodland effect of your terrarium and give your snake a natural solarium for sunning.

The snake you are most likely to start with is some variety of the garter snake Genus *Thamnophis*. They are found throughout the United States, and are so hardy that they can live successfully within the confines of large cities. They vary considerably in color and in pattern. Between the stripes, there may be squares, dots or other geometric markings.

Garter snakes will live for years with proper care but when first introduced into a terrarium, they can be a feeding problem. The first week after you get a garter snake is the crucial time as far as feeding difficulties. In its natural surroundings, garter snakes subsist mainly on frogs, toads and earthworms. Of course, if you are able and whenever you are able, this should be continued and live food should be the first choice for your garter snake. But, during the winter and at other times, this may not be possible and so you should try to teach your garter snake to eat non-living food. With patience, your garter snake will learn to take raw fish and raw meat, such as hamburger and liver. But in the beginning, you may have to resort to strategy and as a last resort, forced feeding, in order to coax the snake to accept non-living food.

As you already know from the eating habits of frogs, one way to make a bit of meat seem to be alive is to dangle it on a string in front of your animal. After a few such feedings, the snake should begin to accept the meat without your bothering to keep it in motion.

A GARTER SNAKE   Philip Gendreau

A SNAKE TERRARIUM

Some herpetologists try to wean the snake away from its natural feeding habits by combining both living and non-living food in a small bowl. They will put a few pieces of meat in a bowl, with a living caterpillar or earthworm in it. The living food will attract the snake and it will usually swallow everything in the dish at the same time.

Should your snake be stubborn, you may have to force it to eat. It is a far simpler operation than you may at first suspect but you must be careful since the mouth of a snake can be easily injured.

You must pamper your snake during this period and you may even use some of the techniques and equipment used for human babies.

Learn to handle your snake properly. Pick it up behind the head. Always support the body by letting it drape itself over your hands or arm. Snakes — just like babies — need to feel they are supported because they are afraid of falling! Use a small stick or toothpick, covered with cotton at one end, to help open the snake's mouth. Mothers often use these Q-tips to clean baby's ears or nose.

Once the snake's mouth is open, force a small bit of fish or meat down the throat, using the cotton swab to push it along. If the snake still refuses to swallow, try massaging the throat with a downward motion.

Another method of forced feeding is to use a medicine dropper, which has a large hole. Sometimes these are used to give babies vitamin drops. Make a fine liquid mixture of chopped meat, water and raw egg. If your mother has a blender, you can get a very smooth consistency that will be easy to come through a medicine dropper. After a few days of forced feedings, your snake should start to adjust to non-living food. If, after a week or two, your snake still refuses to eat under terrarium conditions, you should free it.

Once you set up a feeding schedule, you will only need to feed your snake about once a week. Baby snakes which are in the process of growing may be fed twice a week. In the winter, feed your snake a smaller amount of food, and feed less often, since in nature during the cold months, they do not take any nourishment at all.

SNAKE HUNTS

Garter snakes are so common that you should try to catch your own. Although garter snakes are non-poisonous, you still must exercise certain precautions when going out on a snake hunt. Take the following:

1 — A sturdy pair of hiking boots preferably with rubber soles to prevent slipping on rocks. This will prevent you from being bitten since in your snake hunt you may come across other snakes, which are not quite so harmless.

2 — A basic first aid kit and a snake bite kit.

3 — A cloth drawstring bag to carry home the snakes.

4 — A pair of leather gloves is optional but desirable, if you are in an area where poisonous snakes may be encountered.

One thing that you should anticipate in picking up a frightened garter snake is that it will give off a harmless but horrible-smelling fluid, which is hidden in two glands near the base of the tail. Once it becomes accustomed to your handling, it will discontinue this habit.

Here are a few snakes recommended for beginners:

Ribbon snake *Thamnophis sauritus,* noted as one of the thinnest of American snakes, is an interesting garter snake. The body is generally dark brown or black with three bright yellow stripes, which emphasizes its slenderness. It is swift-moving and eludes its enemies by disappearing from sight underneath aquatic plants. It can swim at the surface of streams or ponds but usually stays close to shore. It eats small frogs, tadpoles, salamanders and small fish but does not like earthworms.

Dekay's or brown snake *Storeria dekayi* is another amazingly thin snake, measuring about a quarter of an inch in diameter, and comparatively small, usually 10-12 inches. It is a live-bearing species. The young are about 4 inches long when born.

It is hardy, gentle in temperament and may be kept in a terrarium with full-grown toads. It has sometimes been called a "city snake" because it has been found within city environs, just as the garter snake.

THE CORAL SNAKE
A beautiful but very
poisonous American snake

THE GARTER SNAKE
It is colorful and
also quite harmless

It was named after James Edward DeKay, a New York naturalist, but is now generally known as the brown snake because of the brown body color.

It enjoys earthworms and may be fed small salamanders, slugs and soft-bodied insects, such as beetles and their grubs.

Smooth-scaled green or grass snake *Liopeltis vernalis* is another slender, gentle snake, which adapts well to terrarium life. Its green coloration is a perfect and protective disguise when it is out hunting insects in the grass. It eats crickets, smooth caterpillars, grasshoppers, spiders and other similar insects. You may want to include a green plant, such as an evergreen or fern, in a flowerpot in a terrarium with a green snake to give it something to climb on and to see how well it blends with the foliage.

Another easy-to-handle snake for the beginner is the eastern ring-necked *Diadophis punctatus,* a small (10-12 inches) woodland snake. Its glossy back comes in variable dark colors, including slate-gray and a blue-black, set off with a yellow neck band. It eats earthworms, small toads, lizards, sala-manders, frogs and even small snakes so it must be kept separated from these creatures. It is a nocturnal animal, withdrawing during the day under leaves, logs or stones.

Eastern hog-nosed snake *Heterodon contortrix* can display a marvelous bagful of tricks to outwit its enemies. It can "play dead" by flipping over on its back. It can puff itself up with air and make a hissing sound, which has given it the name "puff adder" and "hissing adder." It is also known as the "spreading adder" because it can flatten its head and neck, when faced with danger, so that it appears more menacing than it is. It may be said that its hiss is more frightening than its bite because its mouth is kept closed during all of these scare tactics and it rarely bites.

The interesting thing is that nature has provided all of these protective mechanisms since the hog-nosed snake is rather clumsy and slow in movement and it forages for food in open fields and sandy areas, where it is exposed to attack.

The somewhat uncomplimentary epithet "hog-nosed" refers to its hard, turned-up nose, which acts as a shovel in helping it dig up toads, its favorite food.

The family *Elaphe* is commonly called "rat snakes" since the snakes in this group feed principally upon rodents. One of the handsomest of the rat snakes is the corn snake *Elaphe guttata* with bright crimson saddles across its pale red back. It seems to prefer live mice to any other prey and is often found in corn fields where such rodents fare is easily available. However, it will also eat with relish live birds, especially the English sparrow. It lives happily in a terrarium.

TURTLES

Your mother may be afraid of snakes; your sister may not like toads but almost everybody enjoys watching the activities and antics of turtles.

Turtles are hardy, inexpensive and require little care. Water turtles should be kept in a semi-aquatic terrarium where they will have water for swimming and a dry area for sunning. Land turtles require a dry, sandy terrarium with a small bowl, anchored in the sand, for drinking water.

Turtles have a fascinating history. Their family ancestry dates back to the time of the dinosaurs, at least, 150 million years ago. Scientists believe that part of their amazing survival is due to their unusual body structure. The top and bottom of the turtle's body is covered with a protective shell. The top part of the shell is known as the *carapace;* the bottom — the *plastron.*

The names turtle, tortoise and terrapin are often used interchangeably. Some turtle experts try to make fine distinctions. Thus, the word tortoise will be used to designate the terrestrial species that lives only on land; turtles for those that live in the sea, and the name terrapin is given to fresh-water turtles, particularly edible varieties. It is correct, however, for you to call all of these reptiles turtles.

The most popular turtle sold for terrariums is the mobile terrapin or elegant slider *Pseudemys elegans.* They can be purchased at any pet shop for a small sum and can even be found in many five-and-ten cent stores. Some novelty and souvenir shops also sell these turtles with names or designs painted on them. Do not buy these artifically decorated turtles. A

BABY TURTLES HATCHING Philip Gendreau

turtle's shell is made of growing, living tissue. The paint adheres to the shell and stunts its natural development. If you should receive a painted souvenir turtle, scrape off the paint with a knife or razor blade. You can first soften the paint by using a bit of cotton dipped in turpentine or kerosene. Do not use paint remover. Nature's coloring is still the best and the mobile terrapin is noted for its remarkable coloring. The back is green with a border of yellow along the edge. The head and neck are striped with black, green and yellow. There is a bright red mark on each side of the head. Most interesting is the plastron, which is yellow in color, and contains an intricate pattern. No two plastrons are alike. The markings are as varied as snowflakes or fingerprints.

When bought in pet shops, the baby mobile terrapin will be about 2 to 3 inches in length. When fully grown, its shell will measure up to 1 foot in length.

The mobile terrapin is a water turtle. These turtles have webbed hind feet which are adaptable for either walking or swimming. Land turtles are slower moving than water turtles and their feet which are short and stubby have no webbing between them.

Terrapins can swallow only under water which means that their food must be given to them on the surface of the water or else dropped into the water. If you tame them to take food from your hand, they will carry it to the water to eat. Terrapins should not be put in an enclosure with aquarium fish since they will bite or even kill the fish.

Baby turtles should be fed sparingly, once a day. Medium-sized turtles should be fed every other day. Adult turtles do not have to be fed more often than twice a week.

Chop up the food for the baby turtles into small bits. Turtles have no teeth but their jaws have horny edges that can cut sharply into plant or animal food.

You can buy prepared turtle food, which most often consists of dried ant eggs or dried insects. But this kind of diet will prove monotonous for your turtle, as well as lacking in adequate nutrition.

Turtles will eat a wide variety of foods, including meat (raw or chopped beef, chicken, raw hamburger), fish (raw clams, shrimps — and even canned salmon or tuna fish); cheese (firm cheese such as American); and vegetables (they prefer raw leafy green vegetables and are especially fond of lettuce). You can supplement this diet with earthworms and meal worms from time to time.

Although turtles are hardy, they are sensitive to changes in temperature. Turtles are cold-blooded and so the body temperature of a turtle varies with the temperature of its surroundings. A temperature of 75° F. is about right. A temperature drop below 70° F., however, would call for some special attention on your part. During the winter months, if your house should become chilly at night, or in apartment buildings where the heat is cut off or diminished after a certain hour, it is a good idea to put a small electric light a few inches above the terrarium and leave it on all night. You can also keep the electric light on during the day for a few hours should the temperature decline quickly.

It is particularly important to keep a turtle warm during the winter months, otherwise he will become sluggish and inactive. In their natural environment, turtles hibernate during the winter. Sometimes you will find that the first winter you have a turtle, it will attempt to hibernate and will start digging around for a safe sleeping place. If the room temperaure is maintained at a high enough level, however, by the second winter your turtle will have lost this instinct.

MOBILE TERRAPIN
Pseudemys elegans

GOPHER TORTOISE
Gopherus polyphemus

You must be equally cautious about overheating a terrarium with turtles. During the summer should the temperature go above 85° F. make sure that the terrarium is kept in the shade.

If you live near a pond, you may be able to catch your own turtles. Use a net if you are going to hunt for them in the water. On land, you may be able to snatch the small ones by hand. When you pick up a turtle, hold it firmly around the middle of the upper shell. Carry the turtle home in a pail or box. It is not necessary to have water but any covered container should have air holes.

Two land turtles which make good pets are the Eastern box turtle *Terrapene carolina* and the wood turtle *Clemmys insculpta*. Both species, however, are best accommodated in an outdoor turtle pen as living quarters, during the summer months. Since space is usually at a premium, you may not be able to raise your own box or wood turtle but it's interesting to know a little something about them. In the box turtle, the plastron, which is yellow and brown, is hinged near the middle and can be pulled against the upper shell so snugly that the turtle seems boxed in. The box turtle grows to be about 5 inches; the wood turtle averages about an inch or so larger. The carapace of the box turtle is high and arched, a tribute to nature's architectural beauty. The upper shell of the wood turtle is flatter, with a sculptured pattern. Both species eat fresh raw meat and earthworms and enjoy such vegetables as sliced carrots, tomatoes and lettuce and are especially fond of berries.

Two turtles well-adapted for the semi-aquatic terrarium are the painted or "Indian" turtle *Chrysemys picta* and the spotted turtle *Clemmys guttata*.

For a turtle as common as the painted species, it is uncommonly beautiful. The upper shell is smooth, with bright yellow spots on the head. The plastron is yellow or orange, with red spots along the margins; and to complete the painted effect, there are horizontal red stripes on the tail. These vivid colors gives the turtle its name. It is found in large numbers in the northern part of the United States. In its natural habitat, it eats earthworms, small mollusks, and soft-bodied insect larvæ, the aquatic species particularly.

In a home terrarium, it will eat chopped raw meat and fish and as a treat would welcome any of its customary live natural food, which you can obtain for it. As in the instance of the terrapins, it swallows its food underwater.

Spotted turtle or "polka dot" turtle is distinguished by the yellow spots on its black upper shell, neck and head. In feeding and other habits, it is similar to the painted turtle.

If you really want to raise a turtle that has a long and scientifically exciting history, set up a dry terrarium with a gopher tortoise. These turtles are related to the Galapagos Island tortoises, which have been known to grow more than four feet in length, weigh five hundred pounds, and are the largest and oldest of the land turtles.

The gopher tortoise *Gopherus polyphemus* has stumpy club-shaped feet with no webbing, which is characteristic of the land turtle. But it has several unique differences. It has a distinctive, highly arched upper shell with circle-like markings. It owes its name to the fact that it loves to burrow like a gopher. In its natural habitat, it is found largely in the dry parts of the southeastern United States and in the deserts of the southern and southwestern states.

In contrast to the mobile terrapin, the gopher tortoise is strictly a vegetarian. It enjoys a diet of fruits and vegetables.

These turtles should be kept in a terrarium when they are young and small since they attain a shell measurement of 12 inches, and weigh from 9-10 pounds in adulthood.

In time, you'll enjoy telling "fish" tales about the long life of your turtle. Amazing statistics have been quoted about the life span of turtles. Some giant land turtles are said to be over two hundred and fifty years old. The gopher turtle may live to be over one hundred years old. It is interesting to see how long your pet can live. With proper care, your turtle can give you many long years of pleasure.

SPOTTED TURTLE   Philip Gendreau

BABY ALLIGATOR   Lilo Hess-Three Lions, Inc.

ALLIGATORS

The alligator *Alligator Mississippiensis* is the largest living reptile in the United States. It is non-aggressive in character and will rarely attack a man.

Physically, the alligator is admirably outfitted for its semi-aquatic existence. The eyes protrude so they can see above the water level. It has three eyelids: an upper and lower lid, which shuts when it goes to sleep; and a transparent eyelid, which closes the eye from front to back, when the alligator is under water.

THE ALLIGATOR AS A PET

Do not buy a baby alligator for a pet that is over 15 inches long. Usually, you will have to release an alligator to a zoo when it is two years old. By that time an alligator raised in a vivarium will have reached an approximate length of two feet, and weigh an average of three pounds.

The conditions you must provide in order to raise an alligator successfully are:

Housing — Roomy and moist. A baby alligator, measuring no more than 10 inches, may be kept in a 10-15 gallon glass aquarium, partitioned off into a land and water area with a strip of glass, slate or thin board extending across the tank. Use three to four inches of water for the swimming area, and a layer of sand for the land section. The sand should be slightly graded so that it is above water level but do not build it up so high that the alligator cannot climb out onto land easily.

Use a glass cover raised about 1-1½" above the tank to retain moisture. You may also use a triangular shaped metal cover which may be purchased at any aquarium supply store.

As it grows larger, your alligator will need more extensive and elaborate living space.

Feeding — In its natural habitat, the alligator subsists on fish, birds, crabs, earthworms, meat, mice, muskrats and other small animals. With such a varied diet, you have a wide choice of foods to offer it. In a vivarium, it will eat minnows, guppies and earthworms and can be trained to take pieces of raw beef and liver, dangled on a piece of string.

Do not let the wide jaws fool you. Alligators have surprisingly small throats and cannot swallow big pieces of food. What they do is tear their food to bits before swallowing it. The alligator eats in the water but its head is lifted above the water when it swallows.

If a baby alligator refuses to eat for a week or more, you may have to force feed it. Pry open the mouth with a toothpick or match. Push some small bits of raw meat down its throat. A paper drinking straw can help you to ease the food down deeply enough in its mouth so that it will have to swallow. You can also try dangling a worm or minnow in front of the alligator to tempt it. Should it open its mouth, you can then drop the fish in it. Whenever you attempt forced feeding, return the alligator to the water area. Do not press or manipulate the throat or stomach in any way. This hinders, rather than helps, the alligator to swallow.

TEMPERATURE

Alligators enjoy basking in the sun and so the vivarium should be placed on a raised platform or table, where it can get a good measure of sun during most of the day.

A steady temperature of from 75-90° F. day and night should be maintained. Under no condition should the temperature be allowed to drop below 75° F. The swimming water must also be kept warm, at a temperature of 75-80° F. The most efficient way to maintain such an evenly regulated

ADULT ALLIGATOR
Alligator mississippiensis

HEDGEHOG CACTUS
Genus echinocactus

temperature is to use a submergible electric aquarium heater with a separate thermostat.

PLANT TERRARIUMS

A plant terrarium can be started in almost any glass bowl that has a glass cover. If you want to use an unusual or odd-shaped glass container that has no cover, get a glazier to cut a top to size. The glass cover helps retain moisture and cuts down on the frequency of watering the plants. Spraying lightly once a week, or every other week, is adequate. Use a rubber bulb sprayer.

Some plant terrariums, with snug-fitting covers, can go without watering for several months. Although this is possible, most horticulturists suggest that plants should have some air. Thus, the glass top cover should be slightly raised, by slipping pieces of cardboard, cork or rubber "feet" under each corner.

MAKING A GARDEN IN A BOTTLE

A fascinating kind of plant terrarium which will call forth your skill and imagination is the garden in a bottle. It is not as hard to make as you may think.

You can use any type of bottle. However, the demijohn (a narrow-necked bottle, holding from one to ten gallons) is preferred.

The secret is patience, a good selection of small plants that will not be damaged when inserted through the neck of the bottle — and more patience.

The equipment is simple and can be home-made: A funnel of stiff paper; a long, thin tamping stick; a narrow spatula with a long handle for digging. This may be cut from a yardstick or similar piece of wood. Several long, thin rods such as plant stakes to help in the actual planting. A pair of long-handled tongs which may be bought from an aquarium supply shop will also aid in planting.

You will need crushed charcoal, or else a mixture of half peat and half sharp sand for drainage. The soil should be a combination of leaf mold, peat and sand, with one-third rich loam.

Ready, set — go!

Insert the paper funnel in the neck of the bottle, pushing it all the way down to the bottom. The funnel will keep the inside of the bottle free of stirred-up clouds of rising dust. Pour an inch of crushed charcoal down the funnel. Tap the bottle to help the charcoal settle. Dampen the soil before you pour it down the funnel into the bottle. Check that the sides of the bottle are packed firmly. Now is the time to poke around with your long stick. Fill the bottle about a quarter full of soil. Dig holes around the sides of the bottle with your stick. Make the holes large enough for the roots of the plants to fit in easily. With the tongs insert the plants in the bottle. Place the plants that go on the outside border first, then plant the center. Next come the trimmings — the tiny plants that you will use as a ground cover. Small-leaf ivies and baby tears are two recommended ones.

That's it. The first time you do it, you will be amazed at the wonderful results you will be able to achieve — and your friends will be twice as impressed at your ingenuity. You can make an extraordinary thing of beauty just by using ordinary household things around you. The main part of the word *plant* is *plan* — and if you will plan your plant terrarium carefully ahead of time, it will give you great joy for a long time.

Making and maintaining a terrarium, whether plant or animal, can be a rewarding scientific hobby. One of the fascinating sidelights that you will discover as you experiment and try different animal and plant combinations is how closely related animals are — how some of the most common forms of life act and react in an orderly manner. You will also see how animals can learn to adjust to changing environmental conditions. You are doing more than observing animals in a terrarium, you are observing a segment of life. In some ways, the principles you deduce can be applied to yourself and to your relations with the people about you. We, too, must learn to live under changing conditions. We, too, must learn to get along with one another. There is a "U" and an "I" in the word *Universe* and your terrarium may show you the hidden links that bind us all together. Perhaps what you find out in the small glass confined world of your terrarium can be applied to the huge open world we live in. Through the glass window of your terrarium, you may be able to glimpse a broader view of the wonders of the world.

HORNED TOAD AND YOUNG   Lilo Hess-Three Lions, Inc.

THE SCIENCE-HOBBY SERIES

PARTS OF A FROG

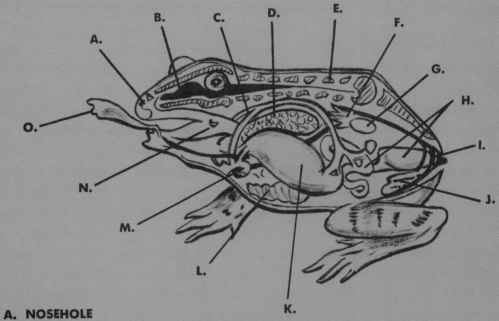

A. NOSEHOLE
B. BRAIN
C. ARTERY
D. LUNG
E. BACKBONE
F. KIDNEY
G. TESTIS
H. INTESTINES
I. VEIN

J. BLADDER
K. STOMACH
L. LIVER
M. HEART
N. OPENING TO VOICE SAC
O. TONGUE

We specialize in publishing quality books for
young people. For a complete list please write

LERNER PUBLICATIONS COMPANY

241 First Avenue North, Minneapolis, Minnesota 55401